Plastic Canvas Kisses

If you love your friends, give them a kiss! These playful pals are called kisses because their mouths can hold one small piece of candy, which makes each little animal (and Clown and Santa) as sweet as a kiss! They're easy to stitch on 7-mesh plastic canvas with worsted weight yarn. Make them for magnets, gift toppers, party favors, stocking stuffers—or just for fun!

Table of Contents

About the Designer

Plastic Canvas Kisses are among the thousands of projects created by the late Dick Martin, a genial and imaginative designer whose friendship we treasured. Dick's publications remain a valued part of the Leisure Arts library. We are pleased to present this sampling of his designs for a new generation to discover and enjoy.

LEISURE ARTS, INC.
Little Rock, Arkansas

2

Deer

Size
4¹/₄"w x 3³/₄"h

Supplies
One 10¹/₂" x 13¹/₂" sheet of 7 mesh plastic canvas
Worsted weight yarn
#16 tapestry needle
12" length of ³/₈"w ribbon

Stitches Used
Backstitch, Gobelin Stitch, Scotch Stitch, Overcast Stitch, and Tent Stitch. Refer to **General Instructions**, pages 31-32, for stitch diagrams.

Instructions
Follow charts to cut and stitch Deer pieces. Matching ▲'s, use tan to join Top to Back along unworked threads. Matching ◖'s, use tan to join Bottom to Back along unworked threads. Tie ribbon in a bow around Deer.

Color Key
▨ white
▨ lt pink
▨ pink
▨ lt tan
▨ tan
▨ black
▨ black 2-ply

Top (12 x 12 threads)

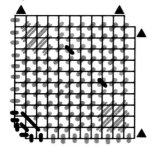

Bottom (12 x 12 threads)

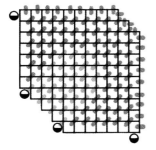

Back (28 x 33 threads)

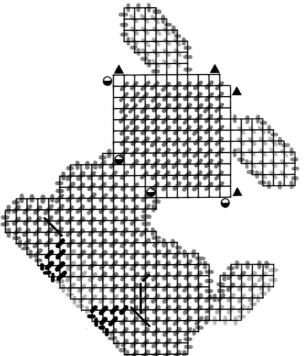

3

Duck

Shown on page 2.

Size
 3³/₄"w x 5"h

Supplies
 One 10¹/₂" x 13¹/₂" sheet of 7 mesh plastic canvas
 Worsted weight yarn
 #16 tapestry needle
 12" length of ³/₈"w ribbon

Stitches Used
 Backstitch, French Knot, Overcast Stitch, Scotch Stitch, and Tent Stitch. Refer to **General Instructions**, pages 31-32, for stitch diagrams.

Instructions
Follow charts to cut and stitch Duck pieces. Matching ▲'s, use yellow to join Top to Back along unworked threads. Matching ◖'s, use yellow to join Bottom to Back along unworked threads. Matching ◆'s and ★'s, use yellow to join Right Wing to Back along unworked threads. Matching ✖'s and ✚'s, use yellow to join Left Wing to Back along unworked threads. Matching ■'s, use white to tack Flower to Back at ■'s. Tie ribbon in a bow around Duck.

Color Key
- ▨ white
- ▨ yellow
- ▨ lt orange
- ▨ pink
- ▨ blue
- ▨ green
- ◉ white Fr. Knot
- • yellow Fr. Knot
- ● pink Fr. Knot
- ◼ black Fr. Knot

Flower (4 x 4 threads)

Left Wing (6 x 7 threads)

Right Wing (7 x 6 threads)

Top (13 x 13 threads)

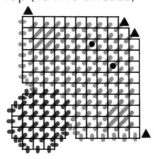

Bottom (13 x 13 threads)

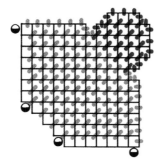

Back (28 x 28 threads)

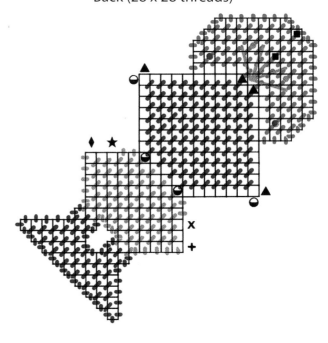

Kitten

Shown on page 2.

Size
3¹⁄₂"w x 4"h

Supplies
One 10¹⁄₂" x 13¹⁄₂" sheet of 7 mesh plastic canvas
Worsted weight yarn
#16 tapestry needle
Clear-drying craft glue

Stitches Used
French Knot, Gobelin Stitch, Overcast Stitch, Scotch Stitch, and Tent Stitch. Refer to **General Instructions**, pages 31-32, for stitch diagrams.

Instructions
Follow charts to cut and stitch Kitten pieces. Matching ▲'s, use lt tan to join Top to Back along unworked threads. Matching ◖'s, use lt tan to join Bottom to Back along unworked threads. Matching +'s, use blue grey to join Bow to Back at +'s. Matching ★'s and ◆'s, use lt tan to join Arm to Back along unworked threads. Matching ✖'s, use lt tan to tack Arm to Bow at ✖'s. Tie an 8" length of blue grey yarn in a bow and trim ends; glue to Top at ✳.

Color Key
⟋	white
⟋	lt pink
⟋	pink
⟋	lt tan
⟍	blue grey
⊙	blue grey Fr. Knot

Top (12 x 12 threads)

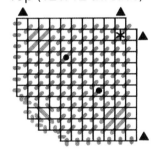

Bottom (12 x 12 threads)

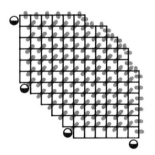

Back (26 x 28 threads)

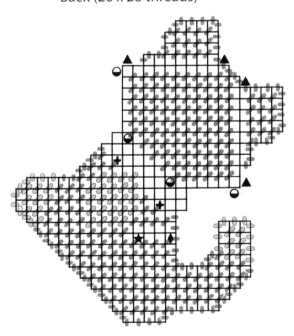

Arm (7 x 9 threads)

Bow (14 x 14 threads)

5

Squirrel

Shown on page 2.

Size
    $4\frac{1}{8}$"w x $3\frac{3}{4}$"h

Supplies
    One $10\frac{1}{2}$" x $13\frac{1}{2}$" sheet of 7 mesh plastic canvas
    Worsted weight yarn
    #16 tapestry needle

Stitches Used
Backstitch, Gobelin Stitch, Overcast Stitch, and Tent Stitch. Refer to **General Instructions**, pages 31-32, for stitch diagrams.

Instructions
Follow charts to cut and stitch Squirrel pieces. Matching ▲'s, use grey to join Top to Back along unworked threads. Matching ◖'s, use grey to join Bottom to Back along unworked threads. Matching ◆'s and ★'s, use grey to join Arms to Back along unworked threads.

Color Key	
▨	ecru
▨	lt pink
▨	pink
▨	lt tan
▨	brown
▨	dk brown
▨	grey
▨	black

Arms (12 x 13 threads)

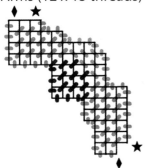

Top (12 x 12 threads)

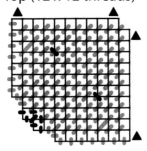

Bottom (12 x 12 threads)

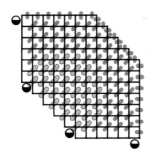

Back (29 x 28 threads)

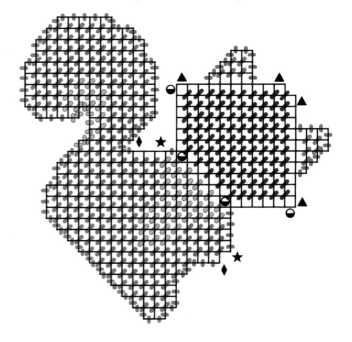

Skunk

Shown on page 2.

Size

3⅞"w x 3¾"h

Supplies

One 10½" x 13½" sheet of 7 mesh plastic canvas
Worsted weight yarn
#16 tapestry needle

Stitches Used

Backstitch, French Knot, Gobelin Stitch, Overcast Stitch, and Tent Stitch. Refer to **General Instructions**, pages 31-32, for stitch diagrams.

Instructions

Follow charts to cut and stitch Skunk pieces. Matching ▲'s, use black to join Top to Back along unworked threads. Matching ◖'s, use black to join Bottom to Back along unworked threads. Matching ◆'s, use blue to tack Bow to Back at ◆'s. Matching ★'s use black to join Arm to Back along unworked threads. Matching ✚'s, use black to tack Arm to Bow.

Color Key	
▨	white
▨	yellow
▨	pink
▨	blue
▨	black
⊙	pink Fr. Knot
⊙	blue Fr. Knot

Arm (9 x 6 threads)

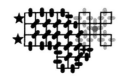

Top (12 x 12 threads)

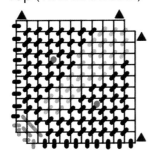

Bottom (12 x 12 threads)

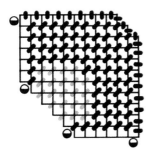

Bow (9 x 9 threads)

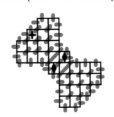

Back (27 x 25 threads)

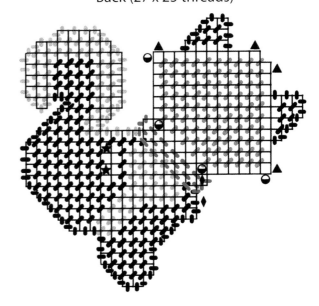

Raccoon

Shown on page 2.

Size
4"w x 3³/₄"h

Supplies
One 10¹/₂" x 13¹/₂" sheet of 7 mesh plastic canvas
Worsted weight yarn
#16 tapestry needle
12" length of ³/₈"w ribbon

Stitches Used
Backstitch, Gobelin Stitch, Overcast Stitch, and Tent Stitch. Refer to **General Instructions**, pages 31-32, for stitch diagrams.

Instructions
Follow charts to cut and stitch Raccoon pieces. Matching ▲'s, use lt beige to join Top to Back along unworked threads. Matching ◒'s, use lt beige to join Bottom to Back along unworked threads. Matching ◆'s and ★'s, use lt beige to join Arms to Back along unworked threads. Tie ribbon in a bow around Raccoon.

Color Key
▨	ecru
▨	orange
▨	pink
▨	blue
▨	lt beige
▨	beige
▨	dk beige
▨	black

Arms (12 x 12 threads)

Top (12 x 12 threads)
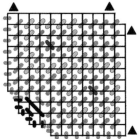

Bottom (12 x 12 threads)
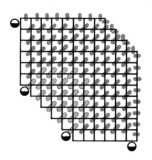

Back (26 x 29 threads)
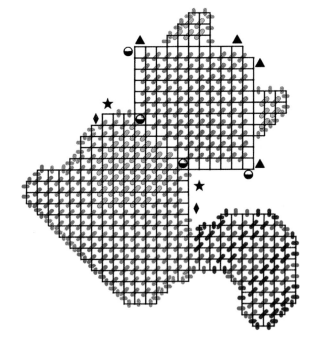

Dog

Shown on page 2.

Size
3³/₄"w x 4"h

Supplies
One 10¹/₂" x 13¹/₂" sheet of 7 mesh plastic canvas
Worsted weight yarn
#16 tapestry needle

Stitches Used
Backstitch, French Knot, Gobelin Stitch, Overcast Stitch, Scotch Stitch, and Tent Stitch. Refer to **General Instructions**, pages 31-32, for stitch diagrams.

Instructions
Follow charts to cut and stitch Dog pieces. Matching ▲'s, use lt tan to join Top to Back along unworked threads. Matching ◒'s, use lt tan to join Bottom to Back along unworked threads. Match ★'s and use brown to join Arm to Back along unworked threads. Matching ◆'s, use white to tack Arm to Back at ◆'s.

Color Key	
⊘	white
⊘	orange
⊘	pink
⊘	lt tan
⊘	brown
⊘	black
●	black 2-ply Fr. Knot

Arm (11 x 11 threads)

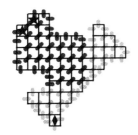

Top (12 x 12 threads)

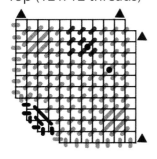

Bottom (12 x 12 threads)

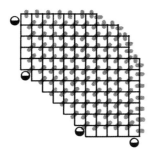

Back (30 x 28 threads)

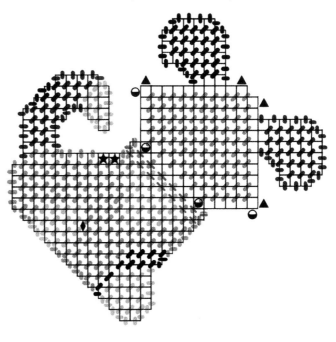

Alligator

Size
3¼"w x 4¼"h

Supplies
One 10½" x 13½" sheet of 7 mesh plastic canvas
Worsted weight yarn
#16 tapestry needle

Stitches Used
Backstitch, French Knot, Gobelin Stitch, Overcast Stitch, Scotch Stitch, and Tent Stitch. Refer to **General Instructions**, pages 31-32, for stitch diagrams.

Instructions
Follow charts to cut and stitch Alligator pieces. Matching ★'s, use green to join Top to Back along unworked threads. Matching ▲'s, use green to join Bottom to Back along unworked threads. Matching ◆'s and ✳'s, use green to join Arms to Back along unworked threads. Matching ◓'s, use orange to join one Flower to Back and Top at each ◓.

Color Key

⊘	white
⊘	orange
⊘	pink
⊘	dk pink
⊘	lt green
⊘	green
⊘	lt tan
⊘	black
●	lt orange Fr. Knot

Top (16 x 16 threads)

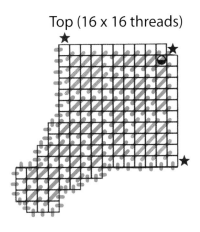

Flower
(4 x 4 threads) (stitch 3)

Arms (13 x 13 threads)

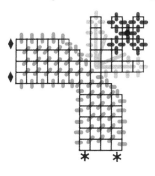

Bottom (16 x 16 threads)

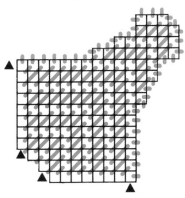

Back (24 x 24 threads)

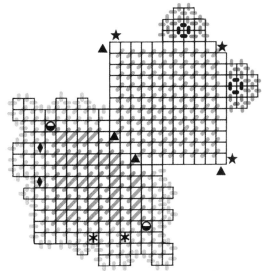

Clown

Shown on page 10.

Size
3¹/₄"w x 4⁵/₈"h

Supplies
One 10¹/₂" x 13¹/₂" sheet of 7 mesh plastic canvas
Worsted weight yarn
#16 tapestry needle
One ¹/₂" red pom-pom
Clear-drying craft glue

Stitches Used
Backstitch, French Knot, Gobelin Stitch, Overcast Stitch, and Tent Stitch. Refer to **General Instructions**, pages 31-32, for stitch diagrams.

Instructions
Follow charts to cut and stitch Clown pieces. Matching △'s, use white to join Top to Back along unworked threads. Matching ⬭'s, use white to join Bottom to Back along unworked threads. Matching ✦'s, use purple to tack Bow Tie to Back at ✦'s. Glue red pom-pom to Top at ◆.

Color Key	
▨	white
▨	red
▨	yellow
▨	green
◪	purple
·	yellow Fr. Knot
⦿	black 2-ply Fr. Knot

Bow Tie (15 x 15 threads)

Bottom (12 x 12 threads)

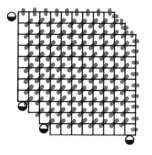

Top (12 x 12 threads)

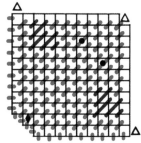

Back (26 x 26 threads)

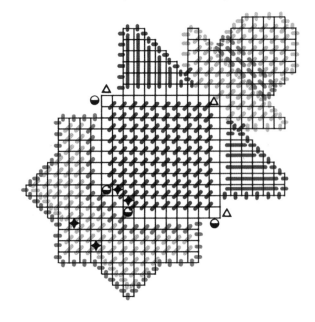

Parrot

Shown on page 10.

Size

4¹/₂"w x 5¹/₈"h

Supplies

One 10¹/₂" x 13¹/₂" sheet of 7 mesh plastic canvas
Worsted weight yarn
#16 tapestry needle

Stitches Used

Backstitch, French Knot, Gobelin Stitch, Overcast Stitch, and Tent Stitch. Refer to **General Instructions**, pages 31-32, for stitch diagrams.

Instructions

Follow charts to cut and stitch Parrot pieces. Matching ★'s, use green to join Top to Back along unworked threads. Matching ▲'s, use green to join Bottom to Back along unworked threads. Matching ◖'s, use green to join Feathers to Back along unworked threads of Feathers.

Color Key

- lt orange
- orange
- dk pink
- green
- ● black 2-ply Fr. Knot

Feathers (10 x 10 threads)

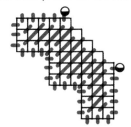

Back (29 x 29 threads)

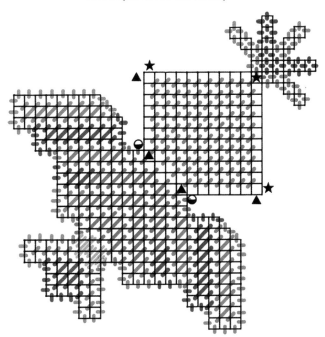

Top (12 x 12 threads)

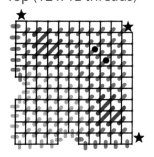

Bottom (12 x 12 threads)

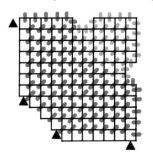

Zebra

Shown on page 10.

Size

3³/₄"w x 4¹/₂"h

Supplies

One 10¹/₂" x 13¹/₂" sheet of 7 mesh plastic canvas
Worsted weight yarn
#16 tapestry needle

Stitches Used

French Knot, Gobelin Stitch, Overcast Stitch, and Tent Stitch. Refer to **General Instructions**, pages 31-32, for stitch diagrams.

Instructions

Follow charts to cut and stitch Zebra pieces. Matching ★'s, use white to join Top to Back along unworked threads. Matching ▲'s, use white to join Bottom to Back along unworked threads. Matching ♦'s and ◒'s, use dk pink to tack Bow Tie to Back at ♦'s and ◒'s.

Color Key	
▨	white
▨	yellow
▨	orange
▨	dk pink
▨	lt tan
◨	black
•	yellow Fr. Knot
⦿	black 2-ply Fr. Knot

Bow Tie (13 x 13 threads)

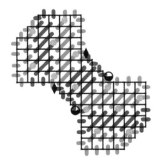

Back (28 x 28 threads)

Top (12 x 12 threads)

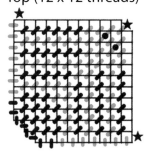

Bottom (12 x 12 threads)

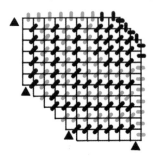

Lamb

Shown on page 15.

Size
3¹/₂"w x 5¹/₈"h

Supplies
One 10¹/₂" x 13¹/₂" sheet of 7 mesh plastic canvas
Worsted weight yarn
#16 tapestry needle

Stitches Used
Backstitch, French Knot, Gobelin Stitch, Lazy Daisy
Stitch, Overcast Stitch, Tent Stitch, and Turkey Loop
Stitch. Refer to **General Instructions**, pages 31-32, for
stitch diagrams.

Instructions
Follow charts to cut and stitch Lamb pieces. Matching
★'s, use white to join Top to Back along unworked
threads. Matching ▲'s, use white to join Bottom to
Back along unworked threads. Matching ◆'s, use
white to tack Left Ear to Back at ◆'s. Matching ✻'s,
use white to tack Right Ear to Back at ✻'s. Matching
◡'s, use lavender to tack Bow Tie to Back at ◡'s. Use
yellow to tack Flower to Back at ✦.

Color Key
▱	white
▱	lt yellow
▱	pink
▰	lt lavender
▱	lavender
▱	pale green
⊙	lt yellow 2-ply Fr. Knot
⊙	pink Fr. Knot
●	lavender Fr. Knot
●	black 2-ply Fr. Knot
⟋	pale green Lazy Daisy
⊙	white Turkey Loop

Left Ear (8 x 7 threads)

Right Ear (7 x 8 threads)

Flower (4 x 4 threads)

Top (12 x 12 threads)

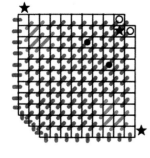

Bottom (12 x 12 threads)

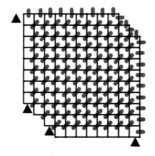

Back (31 x 31 threads)

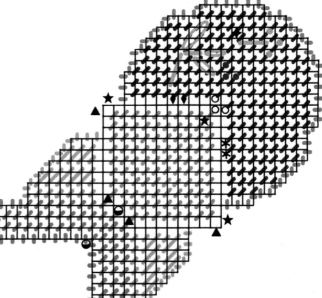

Bow Tie (13 x 13 threads)

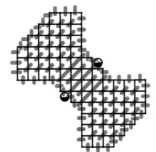

Cow

Shown on page 15.

Size
3⅝"w x 4¾"h

Supplies
One 10½" x 13½" sheet of 7 mesh plastic canvas
Worsted weight yarn
#16 tapestry needle

Stitches Used
Backstitch, French Knot, Overcast Stitch, and Tent Stitch. Refer to **General Instructions**, pages 31-32, for stitch diagrams.

Instructions
Follow charts to cut and stitch Cow pieces. Matching ✚'s, use black to join Top to Back along unworked threads. Matching ◗'s, use black to join Bottom to Back along unworked threads. Matching ▲'s and ✳'s, use red to tack Bandana to Back at ▲'s and ✳'s. Use white to tack Flower to Back at ✦.

Color Key	
⬕	white
⬕	white 2-ply
⬕	pink
⬕	red
⬕	tan
◪	black
⬤	yellow Fr. Knot
⬤	blue Fr. Knot

Bandana (15 x 15 threads)

Flower (4 x 4 threads)

Top (13 x 13 threads)

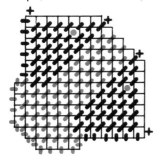

Back (28 x 23 threads)

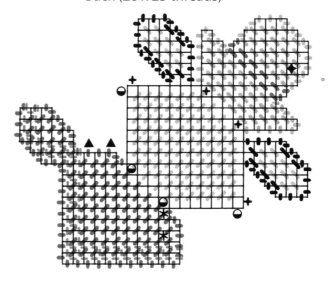

Bottom (13 x 13 threads)

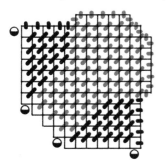

Lion

Shown on page 15.

Size

3¹/₂"w x 5"h

Supplies

One 10¹/₂" x 13¹/₂" sheet of 7 mesh plastic canvas
Worsted weight yarn
#16 tapestry needle

Stitches Used

Backstitch, French Knot, Gobelin Stitch, Overcast Stitch, Scotch Stitch, and Tent Stitch. Refer to **General Instructions**, pages 31-32, for stitch diagrams.

Instructions

Follow charts to cut and stitch Lion pieces. Matching △'s, use tan to join Top to Back along unworked threads. Matching ◕'s, use tan to join Bottom to Back along unworked threads. Matching ◆'s and ★'s, use purple to join Arms to Back along unworked threads. Matching ✳'s, use metallic gold to tack Crown to Back at ✳'s.

Color Key

▨	lt orange
▨	pink
◪	purple
▨	tan
▨	dk tan
◪	black
▨	metallic gold
●	green Fr. Knot
◉	black 2-ply Fr. Knot

Arms (15 x 15 threads)

Crown (8 x 8 threads)

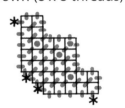

Top (14 x 14 threads)

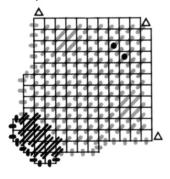

Back (31 x 31 threads)

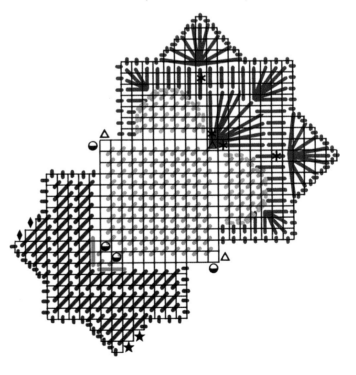

Bottom (13 x 13 threads)

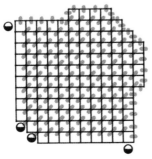

Monkey

Shown on page 15.

Size
3¹/₂"w x 4¹/₈"h

Supplies
One 10¹/₂" x 13¹/₂" sheet of 7 mesh plastic canvas
Worsted weight yarn
#16 tapestry needle

Stitches Used
Backstitch, French Knot, Gobelin Stitch, Overcast Stitch, and Tent Stitch. Refer to **General Instructions**, pages 31-32, for stitch diagrams.

Instructions
Follow charts to cut and stitch Monkey pieces. Matching △'s, use dk tan to join Top to Back along unworked threads. Matching ◖'s, use dk tan to join Bottom to Back along unworked threads. Matching ✱'s and ★'s, use dk orange to join Arms to Back along unworked threads.

Color Key	
◪	white
◪	dk orange
◪	blue
◪	lt tan
◪	dk tan
◪	black
◪	black 2-ply
•	yellow Fr. Knot
⦿	black 2-ply Fr. Knot

Arms (16 x 16 threads)

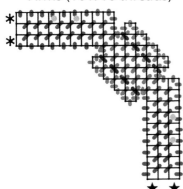

Bottom (12 x 12 threads)

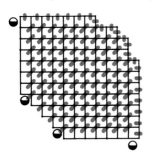

Top (12 x 12 threads)

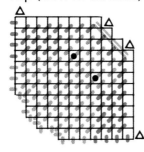

Back (29 x 29 threads)

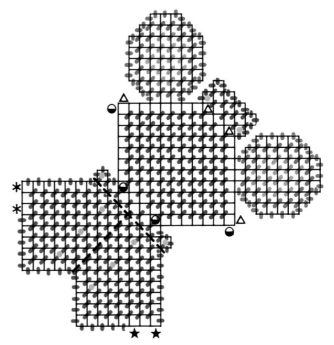

19

Red Dinosaur

Size

2⁵/₈"w x 3"h

Supplies

One 10¹/₂" x 13¹/₂" sheet of 7 mesh plastic canvas
Worsted weight yarn
#16 tapestry needle

Stitches Used

Backstitch, French Knot, Gobelin Stitch, Overcast Stitch, and Tent Stitch. Refer to **General Instructions**, pages 31-32, for stitch diagrams.

Instructions

Follow charts to cut and stitch Red Dinosaur pieces, leaving stitches in blue shaded area unworked. Turn Back over and work stitches in shaded area on opposite side of piece. With wrong sides together and matching ▲'s, place Top on Back. Using red, join Top to Back along unworked edges. With wrong sides together and matching △'s, place Bottom on Back. Using red, join Bottom to Back along unworked edges. Use yellow to tack Flower to Back at ✦.

Color Key

▨	white
▨	yellow
▨	orange
▨	red
▨	green
⊙	orange Fr. Knot
●	black Fr. Knot

Flower (8 x 8 threads)

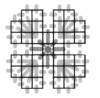

Top (14 x 14 threads)

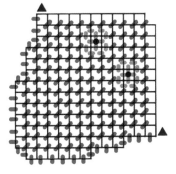

Back (17 x 17 threads)

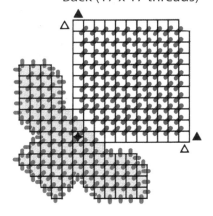

Bottom (14 x 14 threads)

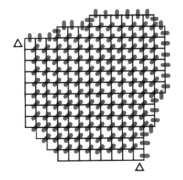

Blue Dinosaur

Size

2⅝"w x 4"h

Supplies

One 10½" x 13½" sheet of 7 mesh plastic canvas
Worsted weight yarn
#16 tapestry needle

Stitches Used

French Knot, Gobelin Stitch, Overcast Stitch, and Tent Stitch. Refer to **General Instructions**, pages 31-32, for stitch diagrams.

Instructions

Follow charts to cut and stitch Blue Dinosaur pieces, leaving stitches in blue shaded area unworked. Turn Back over and work stitches in shaded area on opposite side of piece. With wrong sides together and matching ☆'s, place Top on Back. Using blue, join Top to Back along unworked edges. Referring to photo and matching ◆'s and ◒'s, use blue to tack Crest to Back and Top. With wrong sides together and matching ★'s, place Bottom on Back. Using blue, join Bottom to Back along unworked edges. Use purple to tack Flower to Back at +.

Color Key

▨ white
▨ yellow
▨ purple
▨ blue
▨ green
⦿ yellow Fr. Knot
● black Fr. Knot

Top (16 x 16 threads)

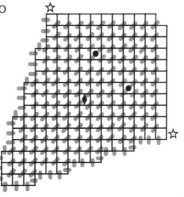

Flower (8 x 8 threads)

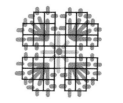

Bottom (16 x 16 threads)

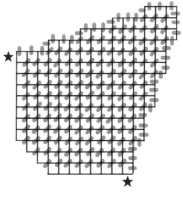

Crest (17 x 14 threads)

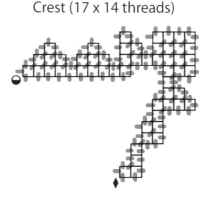

Back (18 x 18 threads)

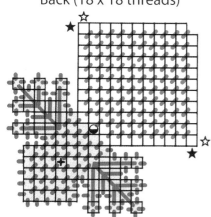

Purple Cow

Size

$3^{1}/_{2}$"w x $4^{1}/_{4}$"h

Supplies

One $10^{1}/_{2}$" x $13^{1}/_{2}$" sheet of 7 mesh
    plastic canvas
Worsted weight yarn
#16 tapestry needle

Stitches Used

Backstitch, Cross Stitch, French Knot, Overcast
Stitch, and Tent Stitch. Refer to **General
Instructions**, pages 31-32, for stitch diagrams.

Instructions

Follow charts to cut and stitch Purple Cow
pieces. Matching ◆'s, use dk purple to join Top
to Back along unworked threads. Matching
◓'s, use dk purple to join Bottom to Back along
unworked threads. Use aqua to tack Flower to
Back at ▲.

Color Key

▨	white
▨	yellow
▨	dk yellow
▨	orange
▨	dk pink
▨	purple
▨	dk purple
▨	aqua
▨	lt green
▨	tan
▨	black
⊙	dk yellow Fr. Knot
⦿	black Fr. Knot

Flower (6 x 6 threads)

Top (13 x 13 threads)

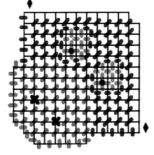

Bottom (13 x 13 threads)

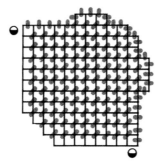

Back (25 x 23 threads)

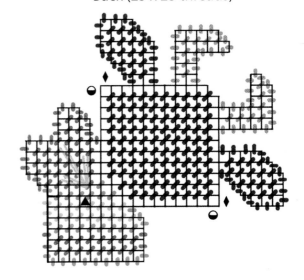

Bunny

Size
$3^1/_4$"w x $4^7/_8$"h

Supplies
One $10^1/_2$" x $13^1/_2$" sheet of 7 mesh plastic
    canvas
Worsted weight yarn
#16 tapestry needle

Stitches Used
Backstitch, French Knot, Gobelin Stitch, Overcast
Stitch, and Tent Stitch. Refer to **General
Instructions**, pages 31-32, for stitch diagrams.

Instructions
Follow charts to cut and stitch Bunny pieces.
Matching ♦'s, use white to join Top to Back
along unworked threads. Matching ◖'s, use
white to join Bottom to Back along unworked
threads.

Color Key
- ▨ white
- ▨ pink
- ▨ purple
- ▨ lt green
- ▧ black
- ◉ pink Fr. Knot
- ◉ yellow Fr. Knot

Back (31 x 30 threads)

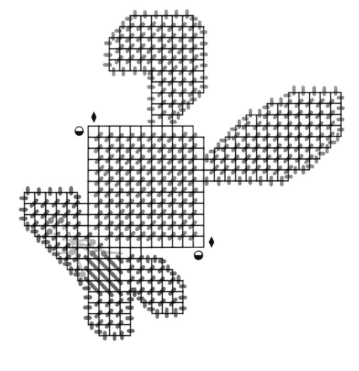

Top (12 x 12 threads)

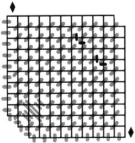

Bottom (12 x 12 threads)

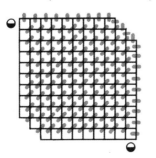

Duck in Straw Hat

Size

$2^5/_8$"w x 4"h

Supplies

One $10^1/_2$" x $13^1/_2$" sheet of 7 mesh plastic
    canvas
Worsted weight yarn
#16 tapestry needle

Stitches Used

Backstitch, French Knot, Gobelin Stitch, Overcast
Stitch, and Tent Stitch. Refer to **General
Instructions**, pages 31-32, for stitch diagrams.

Instructions

Follow charts to cut and stitch Duck pieces.
Matching ♦'s, use white to join Top to Back along
unworked threads. Matching ◖'s, use white to
join Bottom to Back along unworked threads.

Color Key

- ▨ white
- ▨ yellow
- ▨ orange
- ▨ green
- ⦿ black Fr. Knot

Back (24 x 24 threads)

Top (14 x 14 threads)

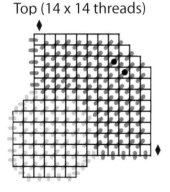

Bottom (14 x 14 threads)

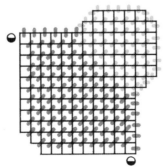

Pig

Size
$3^1/_4$"w x $4^1/_2$"h

Supplies
One $10^1/_2$" x $13^1/_2$" sheet of 7 mesh plastic
canvas
Worsted weight yarn
#16 tapestry needle

Stitches Used
French Knot, Overcast Stitch, and Tent Stitch.
Refer to **General Instructions**, pages 31-32, for
stitch diagrams.

Instructions
Follow charts to cut and stitch Pig pieces.
Matching ♦'s, use peach to join Top to Back
along unworked threads. Matching ◓'s, use
peach to join Bottom to Back along unworked
threads. Matching ★'s, use peach to join Nose to
Top along unworked edges.

Color Key
▨	peach
▨	pink
▨	red
▨	dk purple
▨	aqua
◉	black Fr. Knot

Nose (6 x 6 threads)

Top (12 x 12 threads)

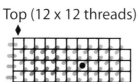

Back (26 x 26 threads)

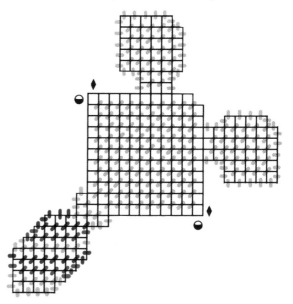

Bottom (12 x 12 threads)

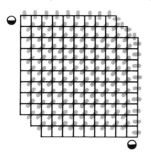

Bright Monkey

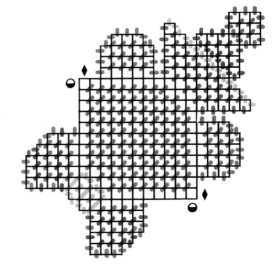

Size

$2\frac{5}{8}$"w x 4"h

Supplies

One $10\frac{1}{2}$" x $13\frac{1}{2}$" sheet of 7 mesh plastic canvas
Worsted weight yarn
#16 tapestry needle

Stitches Used

Backstitch, French Knot, Gobelin Stitch, Overcast Stitch, and Tent Stitch. Refer to **General Instructions**, pages 31-32, for stitch diagrams.

Instructions

Follow charts to cut and stitch Monkey pieces. Matching ♦'s, use gold to join Top to Back along unworked threads. Matching ◖'s, use gold to join Bottom to Back along unworked threads.

Color Key

▨	gold
▨	green
▨	pink
▧	dk pink
▨	dk yellow
▨	orange
⊙	black Fr. Knot

Top (12 x 12 threads)

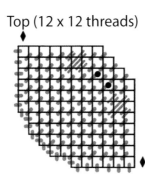

Bottom (12 x 12 threads)

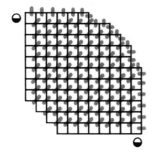

Back (23 x 23 threads)

Speckled Dog

Size

$3^3/_4$"w x $3^3/_8$"h

Supplies

One $10^1/_2$" x $13^1/_2$" sheet of 7 mesh plastic
    canvas
Worsted weight yarn
#16 tapestry needle

Stitches Used

Backstitch, French Knot, Overcast Stitch, and
Tent Stitch. Refer to **General Instructions**,
pages 31-32, for stitch diagrams.

Instructions

Follow charts to cut and stitch Dog pieces.
Matching ♦'s, use white to join Top to Back along
unworked threads. Matching ◖'s, use white to
join Bottom to Back along unworked threads.

Color Key

▨	white
▨	brown
▨	blue
▨	black
●	black Fr. Knot
◉	white Fr. Knot

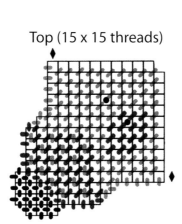

Top (15 x 15 threads)

Back (24 x 24 threads)

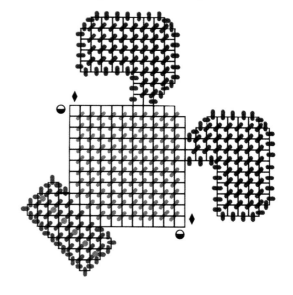

Bottom (14 x 14 threads)

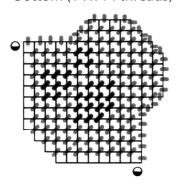

27

Reindeer

Size
$3^1/_2$"w x $4^1/_2$"h

Supplies
One $10^1/_2$" x $13^1/_2$" sheet of 7 mesh plastic canvas
Worsted weight yarn
#16 tapestry needle

Stitches Used
Backstitch, French Knot, Gobelin Stitch, Overcast Stitch, and Tent Stitch. Refer to **General Instructions**, pages 31-32, for stitch diagrams.

Instructions
Follow charts to cut and stitch Reindeer pieces. Matching ♦'s, use gold to join Top to Back along unworked threads. Matching ◓'s, use gold to join Bottom to Back along unworked threads.

Color Key
- ▨ gold
- ▨ tan
- ▨ red
- ▨ black
- ▨ dk green
- ⊙ red Fr. Knot

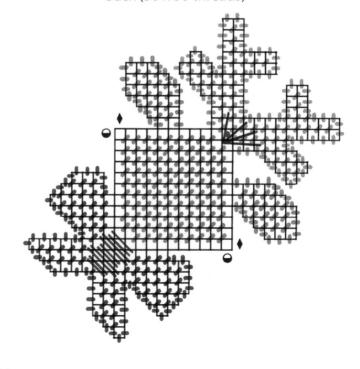

Top (13 x 13 threads)

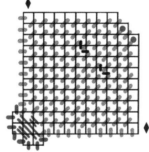

Bottom (12 x 12 threads)

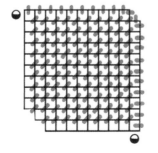

Back (30 x 30 threads)

Santa

Size
3"w x 3½"h

Supplies
One 10½" x 13½" sheet of 7 mesh plastic canvas
Worsted weight yarn
#16 tapestry needle

Stitches Used
Backstitch, French Knot, Fringe Stitch, Gobelin Stitch, Overcast Stitch, and Tent Stitch. Refer to **General Instructions**, pages 31-32, for stitch diagrams.

Instructions
Follow charts to cut and stitch Santa pieces. Matching ◆'s, use white to join Top to Back along unworked threads. Matching ◖'s, use white to join Bottom to Back along unworked threads. Matching ★'s, use red to tack Holly to Back.

Color Key

▨	white
▨	peach
▨	pink
▨	red
▨	dk green
▨	brown
▨	black
⊙	red fringe

Top (12 x 12 threads)

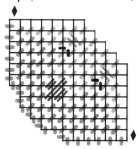

Holly (8 x 8 threads)

Bottom (12 x 12 threads)

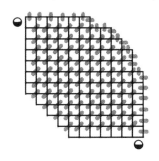

Back (20 x 23 threads)

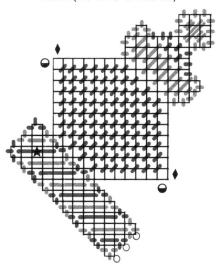

29

General Instructions

Working with Plastic Canvas

Counting Threads. The lines of the canvas are referred to as threads. Before cutting out the pieces, note the thread count of each chart listed near the chart, indicating the number of threads in the width and height. To cut plastic canvas pieces accurately, count **threads** (not **holes**) as shown in **Fig. 1**.

Fig. 1

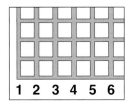

Marking the Canvas. You may use an overhead projector pen to mark the canvas. Outline the shape with pen, cut out, and remove markings before stitching.

Cutting the Canvas. Cut as close to the thread as possible without cutting into the thread. If you don't cut close enough, "nubs" or "pickets" will be left on the edge. Make sure to cut all nubs from the canvas before stitching because nubs will snag the yarn and are difficult to cover. A craft knife is helpful when cutting a small area from the center of a larger piece of canvas. When using a craft knife, protect the table below with a layer of cardboard.

When cutting canvas along a diagonal, cut through the center of each intersection. This will leave enough plastic canvas on both sides of the cut so that both pieces may be used. Properly cut diagonal corners will be less likely to snag yarn and are easier to cover.

Working with Worsted Weight Yarn

Most brands have plies which are twisted together to form one strand. When the instructions indicate two plies of yarn, separate the strand of yarn and stitch using only two of the plies.

Reading the Color Key

A color key is included for each project, indicating the color used for each stitch on the chart. Additional information may also be included, such as the number of plies to use when working a particular stitch.

Reading the Chart

When possible, the drawing on the chart looks like the completed stitch. For example, the tent stitches on the chart are drawn diagonally across an intersection of threads just as they look on the piece. When a stitch cannot be clearly drawn on the chart, like a French Knot, a symbol will be used instead.

Stitching the Design

Securing the First and Last Stitches. Don't knot the end of your yarn before you begin stitching. Instead, begin each length of yarn by coming up from the wrong side of the canvas and leaving a 1"-2" tail on the wrong side. Hold this tail against the canvas and work the first few stitches over the tail. When secure, clip the tail close to the stitched piece. Long tails can become tangled in future stitches or can show through to the right side of the canvas. After all the stitches of one color in an area are complete, end by running the needle under several stitches on the back. Trim the end close to the stitched piece.

Using Even Tension. Keep your stitching tension consistent, with each stitch lying flat and even. Pulling or yanking the yarn causes the tension to be too tight, and you will be able to see through your project. If the tension is too loose, the stitches won't lie flat. Most stitches tend to twist yarn. Drop your needle and let the yarn untwist occasionally.

Joining Pieces

Straight Edges. To join two or more pieces along a straight edge, place one piece on top of the other with right or wrong sides together. Make sure the edges are even, then overcast the pieces together through all layers.

Shaded Areas. Do not work these stitches until the project instructions say you should.

Tacking. To tack pieces, run your needle under the backs of some stitches on one stitched piece to secure the yarn. Then run the needle through the canvas or under stitches on the piece to be tacked in place. This should securely attach pieces without tacking stitches showing.

Uneven Edges. When you join a diagonal edge to a straight edge, the holes will not line up exactly. Keep the pieces even and stitch through the holes as many times as necessary to completely cover the canvas.

Stitch Diagrams

Unless otherwise indicated, bring needle up at **1** and all **odd** numbers and down at **2** and all **even** numbers.

Backstitch

This stitch is worked over completed stitches to outline or define **(Fig. 2)**. It is sometimes worked over more than one thread. It can also be used to cover canvas **(Fig. 3)**.

Fig. 2

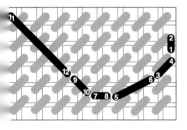

Fig. 3

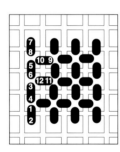

Cross Stitch

This stitch is composed of two stitches **(Fig. 4)**. Cross the top leg of each stitch in the same direction. The number of intersections may vary according to the chart.

Fig. 4

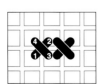

French Knot

Come up at 1. Wrap yarn once around needle. Insert the needle at 2 and pull it through the canvas, holding the yarn until it must be released **(Fig. 5)**.

Fig. 5

Fringe Stitch

Fold a length of yarn in half. Thread needle with loose ends of yarn. Bring needle up at 1, leaving a 1" loop on the back of the canvas. Bring needle around the edge of canvas and through loop **(Fig. 6)**. Pull to tighten loop **(Fig. 7)**. Trim fringe to desired length. A dot of glue on back of fringe will help keep stitch in place.

Fig. 6

Fig. 7

Gobelin Stitch

This straight stitch is worked over two or more threads or intersections **(Fig. 8)**. The number of threads or intersections may vary according to the chart.

Fig. 8

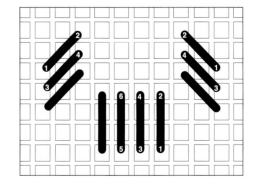

31

Lazy Daisy Stitch

Bring the needle up at 1, make a loop and go down at 1 again. Come up at 2, keeping yarn below needle **(Fig. 9)**. Pull needle through and secure loop by bringing yarn over loop and going down at 3.

Fig. 9

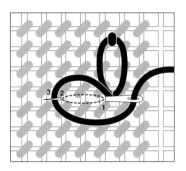

Overcast Stitch

This stitch covers the edge of canvas and joins pieces **(Fig. 10)**. It may be necessary to go through the same hole more than once to get even coverage on the edge, especially at the corners.

Fig. 10

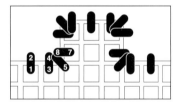

Scotch Stitch

This stitch may be worked over three or more threads and forms a square. **Fig. 11** shows a Scotch stitch worked over three threads.

Fig. 11

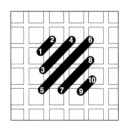

Tent Stitch

This stitch is worked in horizontal or vertical rows over one intersection **(Fig. 12)**. Refer to **Fig. 13** to work the reversed tent stitch.

Fig. 12

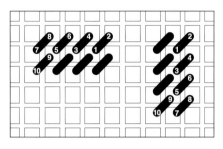

Fig. 13

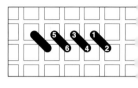

Turkey Loop Stitch

This stitch is composed of locked loops. Bring needle up through hole and back down through same hole, forming a loop on top of the canvas. Make a locking stitch across the thread directly below or to either side of the loop as shown in **Fig. 14**.

Fig. 14

We have made every effort to ensure that these instructions are accurate and complete. We cannot, however, be responsible for human error, typographical mistakes, or variations in individual work.